Culture Is Everywhere

The Museum of Corn-temporary Art

Culture Is Everywhere

The Museum of Corn-temporary Art

Victor Margolin

Photographs by Patty Carroll

Prestel

Munich · Berlin · London · New York

This book is dedicated to the Friends of Corn-temporary Art, who generously contributed to this museum, and to collectors everywhere who have found meaning in their own gatherings of collectible objects.

Front cover: Patty Carroll, Marilyn Monroe figurine

Prestel books are available worldwide. Visit our website at www.prestel.com or contact one of the following Prestel offices for further information.

Prestel Verlag
Königinstrasse 9, 80539 Munich
Tel. +49 (89) 38 17 09-0, Fax +49 (89) 38 17 09-35
e-mail: sales@prestel.de

Prestel Publishing
4 Bloomsbury Place, London WC1A 2QA
Tel. +44 (20) 7323-5004, Fax +44 (20) 7636-8004
e-mail: sales@prestel-uk.co.uk

Prestel Publishing
175 Fifth Avenue, New York 10010
Tel. +1 (212) 995-2720, Fax +1 (212) 995-2733
e-mail: sales@prestel-usa.com

Library of Congress Catalogue Card Number is available.

Editorial direction by Courtenay Smith
Photography assistance: Michele Giffune, Darby Johanson, and Veronica Stein
Research: Kristin Murphy
Lithography by ReproLine, Munich
Printed by Jütte Druck, Leipzig
Bound by Kunst- und Verlagsbuchbinderei, Leipzig

Printed in Germany on acid-free paper

ISBN 3-7913-2760-7

Contents

Culture Is Everywhere: An Introduction to the Museum of Corn-temporary Art

The collector's work as "guardian of past and present" is on view in every museum in the world.[1]

Douglas and Elizabeth Rigby

This book presents the collection of the Museum of Corn-temporary Art, an unusual institution whose objects come from all over the world: hence the book's title *Culture is Everywhere*. While the title indicates the wide geographical sources of the museum's objects, it also asserts that culture is all around us, even in places where we would least expect to find it. In fact, that is the point of the museum. Its collection embraces many things that one might not otherwise think have cultural value.

The Museum of Corn-temporary Art is one of the lesser-known small private museums in the United States. Founded in Chicago in 1988, it comprises about four hundred objects, many of which are showcased in this volume. For the museum's presentation in this book, I invited art historian Hannah Higgins and art critic Hermoine Hartnagel to write critical essays about the collection in order to explore some of the issues it raises. There has been all too little writing about corn-temporary art and these two authors are breaking new ground.

Corn-temporary art is a new category of material culture. It should not be confused with kitsch, which scholars and critics have tended to characterize in a patronizing or derogatory way.[2] The art critic Clement Greenberg, in his seminal essay, "Avant-Garde and Kitsch" of 1939, defined kitsch as follows:

Kitsch is mechanical and operates by formulas. Kitsch is vicarious experience and faked sensations. Kitsch changes according to style, but remains always the same. Kitsch is the epitome of all that is spurious in the life of our times. Kitsch pretends to demand nothing of its customers except their money—not even their time.[3]

Curators Kirk Varnedoe and Adam Gopnik were more forgiving in their exhibition *High & Low* at the Museum of Modern Art in 1990. Softening Greenberg's harsh judgment of kitsch, they referred instead to "low" art which modern artists from Pablo Picasso to Robert Rauschenberg incorporated in their paintings and sculptures.[4] According to Varnedoe and Gopnik, low art could be raised to another level through the operation of superior aesthetic judgment. Jeff Koons, associated with the post-modern attempt to break down the division between high and low art, pushed this argument to the edge with his outsized versions of objects otherwise considered to be kitsch. He managed to erase most traces of high art in his *Michael Jackson and Bubbles* (1988), a gilded statue of Michael Jackson and his monkey as well as his gigantesque *Pink Panther* (1988), both of which have nonetheless been shown as examples of high art in museums throughout the world. Within the polarization of high and low, corn-temporary art would normally be associated with the low since it is a popular art whose exemplars, unlike the art of Jeff Koons, are mostly inexpensive multiples. However, the Museum of Corn-temporary Art rejects the high/low distinction and prefers an independent system of judgment for its collection. Corn-temporary art arises from conditions of use and must be considered in terms of its social value as well as its visual qualities. It refuses the appellation "kitsch" because it is neither bereft of significance nor short on aesthetic value. Cornnoisseurs of corn-temporary art are like the enthusiasts of Pop described by British historian and critic Reyner Banham: "A Pop Art connoisseur is opposed to a fine art connoisseur. The opposition, however, is only one of taste, otherwise the training required to become a connoisseur is the same."[5]

Qualities of Corn-temporary Art

The taste for corn-temporary art is based on two factors, one social and the other aesthetic. Because this art reveals a great deal about human values as they are filtered through systems of production, it belongs to the pool of material artifacts that constitute cultural gestalts. Often politically and socially incorrect, it represents the dark side of material culture, which is so pervasive that evidence of it can hardly be swept under the metaphoric rug. Figures of sleeping Mexicans, for example, can still be found in Mexican souvenir stalls and in shops on the U.S. side of the border. Despite their stereotypical representation, they continue to be produced for tourists.[6] Consider also, the supine female nude whose breasts function as salt-and-pepper shakers or the male body-builder whose firm buns serve the same purpose. Although they are regarded as offensive by some, they circulate widely as jokes in material form. Whether or not we appreciate corn-temporary art, it makes us more conscious of how the full range of human values is embedded in material culture.

Although corn-temporary art has as much power to explain the social values and practices of the recent past as flints and axes do for the earliest human societies, it is still the bastard child of material culture and is rarely displayed in museums of history or ethnography.[7] There is more than one reason for this. First, corn-temporary art is frequently produced on a small scale and appears inconsequential compared to larger objects such as utensils or furniture in a history museum vitrine. However, lets consider the importance of the period in a writing system. As an object, the period is infinitesimal compared to the size of a letter but it plays a powerful role in the text. In short, it prevents one sentence from running into another. Similarly corn-temporary art objects, while generally diminutive in scale, are powerful

bearers of meaning that establish boundaries for cultural concepts just as a period defines the length of a sentence. But they are rich in aesthetic value too and thus transcend the limits of ethnographic discourse. As Banham noted, the aesthetic codes of popular art may be different from those of high art, but they are no less complex, whether one is looking at formal aspects or iconography.

One difference between corn-temporary art and high art is the materials the former is made of. Unlike the tradition of decorative art that bases the aesthetic value of an object in part on the richness or fineness of its material, corn-temporary art is produced with the cheapest of materials such as plastic, wood, and lead. It derives its aesthetic virtue from the way those materials are manipulated to create an object's meaning. Within the Museum of Corn-temporary Art's collection, for example, are a number of small chairs and stools made from Pepsi and other soda cans. Their "beauty," is achieved by transforming a cheap aluminum alloy into an elegant object. The folk artists who make such furniture are skilled at curling aluminum cans to achieve decorative effects, thus drawing an otherwise "low" material into a new aesthetic orbit. Or, think of the cheap ceramic salt-and-pepper shakers that were originally made in Japan and are now produced all over the world. They are a popular version of the more elite Meissen figurines of the eighteenth century, and the strong semantic value of their subject matter, whether Dutch couples kissing on skates or dogs urinating on hydrants, draws the cheap clay they are made of into a higher realm of meaning than would otherwise be achievable.

In attempting to straddle the social purpose of the ethnography museum and the aesthetic agenda of the art gallery, corn-temporary art falls between two stools. In the ethnography museum, it challenges the more ponderous methods of constructing social meanings with objects that represent conventional cultural categories—bows and arrows, hand tools, furniture, pottery, dolls, musical instruments, and writing implements.[8] Or else it counters the sacred significance of ritual objects such as masks and chalices. The image of a culture that we usually find in an ethnography museum is one bereft of corn-temporary art, which does not fit easily into the conventional categories of daily life or sacred ritual.

Likewise, corn-temporary art defies the collecting conventions of art museums and galleries. First, it is anonymous. Almost nothing is known of any corn-temporary artists. When recognized artists or designers do produce objects in a corn-temporary genre such as the souvenir, their work is immediately recontextualized as high art. This is the case of the ironic souvenirs created by the New York designers, Constantine and Lauren Boym. Depicting unbuilt monuments and buildings associated with disasters, they were shown in the Whitney Biennale several years ago.[9] Even when artists use corn-temporary art as "found" objects, the original meaning and aesthetic of the objects are subordinated to the way the artist employs them in high art installations for personal expression or social commentary.

The aesthetic of corn-temporary art is generally found wanting by high art curators who only tolerate vernacular forms when they are either incorporated aesthetically into high art objects as the artists in Varnedoe's and Gopnik's *High & Low* show did, when they are used by contemporary artists who eschew formal aesthetics for intellectual irony, or when they are presented in categories such as "outsider art" as the production of recognized "outsider artists." Design curator Ellen Lupton has challenged this paternalistic view of the vernacular in her discussion of how the binaries of low and high operate in graphic design. "The conflict between low and high," she writes, "is not a matter of content but of structure. Low and high is a pattern, a conceptual shell, whose value shifts from situation to situation. What is high in one setting is low in another...The term 'vernacular,' like the high/low pair, is relative: it positions a standard language against a lesser dialect, a dominant culture against a secondary subculture."[10] To counter this problem of binaries, a new museum is urgently needed to provide a showcase for the vast aggregate of corn-temporary art objects that are so unwelcome elsewhere.

The Birth of the Museum

The impetus to found the Museum or Corn-temporary Art was a small Greek ouzo bottle housed in a frame of plastic caryatids and capped with a top in the shape of an Ionic column. The bottle was literally rescued from the gutter where it had most likely been cast by an inebriated reveler. The incentive for retrieving it was an overwhelming feeling of aesthetic pleasure. For months it stood mutely on a shelf, inarticulately evoking this feeling but revealing nothing of its own workings. Only gradually did the elements of a corn-temporary aesthetic begin to emerge. The beauty of the bottle was derived from the way classical Greek iconography, previously associated with temples and monuments, had been dissected, miniaturized, and then transposed onto it. Elegant marble was transmuted into common plastic. A capital was severed from its architectural setting and transformed into a bottle top. The bottle reeked with the grandeur of Greece's classical heritage. What was so intriguing was the quality of the aesthetic moves that produced it. The ouzo bottle revealed a sincere desire to embed the majesty of Greek culture in a form that that could circulate widely and reach people from all walks of life.

Once the characteristics of a corn-temporary aesthetic had become clear, myriad objects presented themselves as candidates for inclusion in this new category. Travels far and wide made possible visits to souvenir stores, flea markets, junk shops, antique malls, and other sites where such objects are bought and sold. Sometimes they are offered for sale as "collectibles," but often they appear as inconsequential agglomerations of matter, waiting patiently to be yanked from the dustbin of history and reinstated as objects of cultural worth. At first, the acts of acquiring such objects seemed to be simply the indulgence of a junk snupper's private passion. And as the acquisitions accumulated, they fit no conventional categories of collecting. Although some might have been placed in existing categories of collectibles such as "salt-and-pepper shakers" or objects "Made in Japan," they were not procured for that reason nor did the collecting process take on the compulsion of the serial collector who, once he or she identifies a category of collectibles, must fill that category with as many exemplars as possible.[11]

The eclecticism of the purchases was, in fact, troubling since they made no sense as a collection.[12] The acquisition process was in no way comparable to the amassing of snuff boxes, hat pins, or cookie jars. Soon it became evident that the only way to continue the collection was to house it in a museum where its cultural meaning could be explored through the conventional scholarly practices of exhibition, research, and publication.

As the objects accumulated, it became necessary to consider the problem of classification, since their growing volume was becoming disorderly and confusing. Unfortunately, there were no models to draw from except the structural model of museum administration. According to this model, artifacts are allocated to departments, each of which is managed by knowledgeable curators. Although the departmental model eventually seemed most reasonable, it was not entirely satisfactory since there were no existing categories of corn-temporary art to emulate, nor were there trained experts to staff the departments. Nonetheless, for the sake of credibility as much as for the need to impose some sort of order on an unruly mass of materiality, the departmental model was adopted. Although it works well administratively by recognizing the importance of subdividing a collection in order to attend to it effectively with appropriate expertise, it provides little guidance as to what the content of each subdivision should be. Expertise in ethnography is generally recognized in terms of specific geographic areas. Thus ethnographic collections are usually grouped according to where the artifacts originated—Africa, South Asia, the Near East or elsewhere. Art museums also make distinctions between geographic areas but they use other criteria such as chronology and medium. Thus a comprehensive art museum would have a department of ancient art, one for European art between 1400 and 1800, and another for American decorative art. As well, there might be departments that are organized by media—prints and drawings, photography, design, and costume.

Such departments were considered carefully. Several, notably decorative art, design, and fashion, fit the Museum of Corn-temporary Art. But many of the museum's objects belong to typologies that do not exist in art or ethnography museum collections. Therefore new departments had to be devised. After rejecting geography and chronology as viable subdivisions, it seemed that function or purpose would best organize much of the collection, including those groupings of objects such as clothing and decorative art that paralleled established art museum categories. In the end, seven departments were created: souvenirs, decorative art, folk art, commercial art, design, icons, and fashion. Although the departmental strategy does have problems since some objects fit the criteria of more than one department, its advantage is that it foregrounds the way that objects are used by the people who acquire them. A souvenir, for example, may also serve as a decorative art object on a shelf or mantlepiece but this does not mean that it doesn't still evoke memories of a trip to Florida or Australia. A pair of salt and pepper shakers may grace a living room shelf or just as well end up on the dinner table where the family sprinkles their meat loaf with salt from the head of a pigtailed Chinaman.

Exhibit Strategies

The display strategy in *Culture is Everywhere* is twofold. First, objects are presented according to the departments where they are housed. But the Museum of Corn-temporary Art also has a policy of curating across the collection and its exhibits tackle large themes such as the nature of masculinity and femininity and the representation of national identity. A word must also be said here about the presentation strategy of the collection. Both Patty Carroll and I have decided that the best way to exhibit corn-temporary art, whether as representative of the collection or in themed exhibits, is to use an aesthetic similar to that of the objects themselves. While some objects have been photographed against single-colored backgrounds in order to better reveal their multifarious details, others have been installed in narrative settings. The intent of these settings is not to trivialize the objects by surrounding them with a "cute" decor but rather to use the decor to enhance the visual pleasure the objects are meant to evoke without compromising their iconic power.

The Future of the Museum

The Museum of Corn-temporary Art's long-range plan includes three major goals. The first is to continue building the collection and perhaps even expand into new areas. While the current departmental structure is solid, additional departments will be created as the need arises. For example, the museum has amassed a miscellaneous body of visual imagery that may require a Department of Prints in the future.

The second goal is to find a permanent home for the museum. It does not yet have its own building but a possibility exists to convert the Grecian Holiday Motel, an abandoned structure in southern Illinois. As a prime example of

Cornucopia

LES MAIN-COURSES

Gogh au Van with Kokoshka varnishkes
and Georges bracquoli

Omlette au duchampignons

Rigatoni Shafrazi

Eggplant Parmigianino with Haricorot vert

LES DESSERTS

Courbet sorbet

Donatello jello

COCKTAILS AT THE ALFRED BAR

Magritta: A Surrealist Surprise

Menu for the Cornucopia, the five-star restaurant planned for the Museum of Corn-temporary Art's new home.

the Greek Revival Motel style, the Grecian Holiday is graced with a number of features such as caryatid gas pumps, which make it an excellent example of corn-temporary architecture. Along with exhibition spaces, offices, a library, and gift shop, plans call for the creation of a five-star French restaurant, tentatively titled the Cornucopia. Along with the restaurant will be the Alfred Bar, which will serve an innovative range of corn-temporary cocktails including one conceived especially for the museum, the Magritta.

And lastly, there is a need to exhibit the collection more extensively. Corn-temporary art has much to contribute to the cultural milieu. To use the terms of Stephen Greenblatt, a prominent scholar of English Literature, the collection is filled with "resonance" and "wonder." "By resonance," Greenblatt writes, "I mean the power of the displayed object to reach out beyond its formal boundaries to a larger world, to evoke in the viewer the complex, dynamic cultural forces from which it has emerged and for which it may be taken by a viewer to stand. By wonder I mean the power of the displayed object to stop the viewer in his or her tracks, to convey an arresting sense of uniqueness, to evoke an exalted attention."[13]

Although the idea of corn-temporary art will be new to readers of this book, many of the objects herein will be familiar. They will have been previously understood as cheap artifacts of a global culture that disgorges commodities indiscriminately and endlessly. The aim of the Museum of Corn-temporary Art is to rescue these objects from that perception and re-present them in a context where their resonance and wonder can enhance our sense of what it means to be human.

Victor Margolin
Director, The Museum of Corn-temporary Art

1 Douglas and Elizabeth Rigby, *Lock, Stock and Barrel: The Story of Collecting* (Philadelphia, New York, and London: J.B. Lippincott, 1944), 477.

2 See Gillo Dorfles, *Kitsch: The World of Bad Taste* (New York: Universe Books, 1969), Matei Calinescu, "Kitsch" in Calinescu, *Five Faces of Modernity: Modernism, Avant-Garde, Decadence, Kitsch, Postmodernism* (Durham: Duke University Press, 1987), and Thomas Kulka, *Kitsch and Art* (University Park: Pennsylvania State University Press, 1996).

3 Clement Greenberg, "Avant-Garde and Kitsch," in Greenberg, *Art and Culture: Critical Essays* (Boston: Beacon Press, 1961), 10.

4 Kirk Varnedoe and Adam Gopnik, *High & Low: Modern Art, Popular Culture* (New York: Museum of Modern Art, 1990)

5 Reyner Banham, "Who is this 'Pop'?" in Reyner Banham, *Design by Choice*, ed. Penny Sparke (London: Academy Editions, 1981), 94.

6 For a complex discussion of the meaning of the sleeping Mexican, see Paul Rich and Guillermo De Los Reyes, "Mexican Caricature and the Politics of Popular Culture," *Journal of Popular Culture* 30 no. 1 (Summer 1996): 133–145. Rich and De Los Reyes suggest that the sleeping Mexican, whom they call the sombreroed dozer, may not be lazy but instead a representation of indifference by the peasant class to the corruption and lack of attention to their needs by the PRI, the party that until the election of Vicente Fox had ruled Mexico since 1929.

7 As an exception, in March 2000 the Jewish Museum of Maryland opened an exhibition entitled *Tchotchkes! Treasures of the Family Museum*, which featured a large assemblage of Jewish knickknacks ("tchotchke" means knickknack). The exhibition's intent was to treat the material as a serious form of popular culture.

8 A good example of an ethnography museum is the Pitt Rivers Museum in Oxford, England. Pitt Rivers' typological classification of artifacts influenced ethnography museums worldwide for sixty or seventy years from the time he gave his collection to Oxford in 1883.

9 See Constantine Boym, "Missing Monuments" and "By Design" in *Metropolis* (November 1995), 35, 39 and 34, 37, 39. Boym incorporates the souvenir into a fine art hierarchy when he argues that "[i]ts time for designers to honor them [souvenirs] properly, by reinventing that tired, hackneyed representation of a civilization's heritage—the souvenir." (37)

10 Ellen Lupton, "Low and High: Design in Everyday Life," in Ellen Lupton and J. Abbott Miller, *Design Writing Research: Writing on Graphic Design* (New York: Princeton Architectural Press, 1996), 157.

11 For a good example of a serial collection, though one gathered with a curatorial sense of representing diverse building types, see Margaret Majuda and David Weingarten, *Souvenir Buildings, Miniature Monuments: From the Collection of Ace Architects* (New York: Harry N. Abrams, 1996). The collection of Majuda and Weingarten has more than 2,400 exemplars and is still growing.

12 A number of objects have also been contributed to the museum by the Friends of Corn-temporary Art, a loose-knit group to whom this book is dedicated.

13 Stephen Greenblatt, "Resonance and Wonder," in *Exhibiting Cultures: The Poetics and Politics of Museum Display*, eds. Ivan Karp and Steven D. Lavine (Washington and London: Smithsonian Institution Press, 1991), 42.

The Museum

Department of Souvenirs

Souvenirs comprise the largest category of artifacts in the Museum of Corn-temporary Art's collection. The souvenir is a product of tourism and was invented as a response to the traveler's desire to take home a memory or token of a destination he or she had visited. Such a desire has many motives: to remember a particular experience that is connected to a place; to show others that one has been to that place; and to affirm one's own identity as a traveler. Souvenirs are produced as forms of revenue and for the most part are intended to embody "typical" images associated with a place. However, as objects in this department make clear, souvenirs are sometimes anomalies. Miniature German beer steins sold as souvenirs of New Mexico are good examples. What makes the study of souvenirs particularly interesting is the process by which these typical images are created and then continue to be manufactured at dispersed sites of production without any formal agreement as to their representational veracity. In Florida, for example, alligators are prominent icons while in Paris, the quintessential icon is the Eiffel Tower, which can represent either the city or France as a nation.

Snowdomes

According to knowledgeable collectors, snowdomes have been around since the 1880s. They go under various names such as "snowglobe," "snowball," "show-shaker," and "Shake 'n snow." Snowdomes are souvenir forms used by cities and tourist destinations around the world, even those where there is no snow. Originally they took various forms such as small cubes and bottle shapes. Today, almost all are rounded plastic domes that contain images of buildings, artifacts, or activities associated with a particular place.

Slave Watchtower

Before the Cuban Revolution in 1959, different regions of Cuba had their own souvenirs for tourists. In the Valle de los Ingenios (Valley of the Sugar Mills) near Trinidad is the 44-meter-high slave watchtower on the Manaca Iznaga estate. It is the principal representation of Trinidad in this pre-revolutionary souvenir.

Cuban Souvenirs

Cuba claims to be free of racism yet some of its souvenirs are questionable ethnic representations. The four seated figures in this image are similar to the Three Wise Monkeys, yet their more human features result in a derogatory depiction of black people, comparable to the coon images found in American culture in earlier times.

Sleeping Mexicans

The sleeping Mexican remains an archetypical and complex image of Mexican identity. Not only does it circulate in the form of souvenirs, but it also serves as a logo for many Mexican restaurants outside Mexico. While it would seem to signify a lazy person, according to some interpretations it suggests the peasant's resistance to politicians who seek to exploit him.

Mexican Ruins

The archeological sites of ancient Mexican cultures are primary tourist attractions and as iconic objects or monuments they are miniaturized for consumption. These include the giant Olmec head, the Mayan pyramid at Chichen Itza, and the Mayan reclining figures known as Chacmools.

Mexican Burros and Campesino

The burro and the campesino weighed down with baskets are frequently depicted in Mexican souvenirs and popular art. Such images endure despite the social and economic changes that have modernized large parts of Mexico.

Statue of Liberty

The Statue of Liberty is not only a New York landmark, it is an American symbol. A gift from France to the United States, it has greeted immigrants from its pedestal on Ellis Island since 1885. As a New York souvenir, it is the dominant icon, far stronger than the Empire State Building.

Washington D.C. Capitol and Washington Monument

The United States Capitol and the Washington Monument are classic souvenir icons of Washington D.C. However, few people today are aware that the monument was constructed to honor George Washington. Instead, it has come to signify the city of Washington rather than the man it was intended to commemorate.

Alaskan Souvenirs

In the past, native peoples of the Northwest United States and Canada were represented by stereotypes of Eskimos and others but these have been replaced for the most part by souvenirs such as miniature totem poles, which are intended to replicate more closely genuine cultural artifacts

Florida Souvenirs

As a vacation spot, Florida has a long history of souvenir production. Its tropical landscape and exotic fauna, notably alligators and flamingos, are pervasive on ashtrays, as salt and pepper shakers, and in snowdomes. Shells are also closely associated with Florida memories and are used extensively for a variety of souvenirs.

Gulls and Lobster Traps

Gulls are usually paired with lobster traps, buoys, or driftwood to sustain memories of seaside vacations.

Tiki Figures

Tiki mugs, salt and pepper shakers, and vases are artifacts from a commercial culture that probably originated in the mid 1950s. Some of the figures draw inspiration from the huge Moai heads of Easter Island while others represent pastiche notions of Polynesian deities. The Easter Island style is evident in some objects, but others draw from sources as far afield as African masks and Northwest Coast totem poles. Many are simply copies of other pastiches.

Manneken Pis Figures

The Manneken Pis, a bronze statue of a little boy peeing, is the
most popular monument in Brussels and is emblematic of the city's
identity. The city museum has more than 600 costumes that have
been made for the figure who is garbed in one or another of them
on special occasions. There are various legends as to the figure's
origin. One has it that during the Crusades a little boy put out a
threatening fire in Brussels by urinating on it. Another states that a
wealthy man had lost his son and after two days found the boy
peeing close to the place where the statue now stands. Out of grat-
itude, he had the fountain of a peeing boy constructed. The Manneken Pis has been produced in a number of versions including several where he has an erection and one, found in Hong Kong, where
his penis ejects a flame to light a cigarette.

Dutch Figures

Dutch souvenirs play on the mythical conventions of national identity—wooden shoes, windmills, and folk costumes as embodied in childrens' stories such as "Hans Brinker and the Silver Skates." Modern Dutch cities, though replete with excellent architecture and monuments, have been unable to produce comparable souvenir icons to compete with these traditional folk images.

Sami Souvenirs

The Sami people, also called Lapps, inhabit the northernmost parts of Finland, Sweden, and Norway. Until recently, reindeer herding was the basis of the Sami economy. Now tourism has become a major business. Sami souvenirs derive mainly from their dress – tiny fur shoes, Sami dolls in folk costume, and then also wearable items like gloves. More obscure is the miniature food storage hut, which requires some knowledge of Sami culture to appreciate it. The Sami figure in the photograph was made by a folk artist in Karashok, Norway.

Slovenian Souvenirs and Irish Figures

Small Slovenian souvenirs include a wooden rack for drying hay and a wine vat. Even though Slovenia is working hard at modernization, its souvenirs depict agrarian artifacts, rather than urban objects, as national icons. The Irish figures in green are also represented in a nostalgic country style.

Berlin Wall and Valise

After the Berlin Wall came down, entrepreneurs were quick to produce souvenirs that incorporated pieces of it. At bottom left is a boxed tableau that sets a piece of the Berlin Wall, an East German coin, and an upended Trabant or Trabi, the small East German car, against a view of the Brandenburg Gate, an icon of West Berlin. At the top is a liquor flask in the form of a suitcase and at bottom right, a small ceramic container from Meissen, where the great German porcelain factory was founded in the 18th century.

Beer Steins

Beer steins are identified historically with Germany and miniature ceramic steins have become typical German souvenirs. But they have served the same function with local imagery in New Mexico, Arizona, and Florida, thus provoking cross-cultural confusion for the sake of commerce.

New Mexico Beer Steins

In these souvenir salt and pepper shakers from New Mexico, the beer stein is used simply as a convenient backdrop for a local landscape, even though it bears no relation to Southwestern culture.

Eiffel Tower

Since its construction as part of the World Exposition of 1889, the Eiffel Tower, designed by the French engineer, Gustave Eiffel, has become a symbol of Paris and French nationhood. Today, few people recall its original meaning as a signifier of French technological prowess. Instead it has become an abstract marker of Paris as a tourist destination and a sign of Frenchness for bakeries, nightspots, and cafes. It equates Paris with sensual pleasure when it is used for perfume bottles or liquor decanters.

Italian Souvenirs

In Italy, regionalism is strong and no cultural icon represents the country in the way the Eiffel Tower does in France. In Milan, the cathedral is the emblematic building, while in Rome it is the Coliseum and in Pisa the Leaning Tower. In Sicily, where folk traditions are still strong, the horse-drawn painted wagon represents the island's character, while in Urbino, it is not a building or object that characterizes the town but the images of the Duke and his consort, which have been memorialized in the fifthteenth-century paintings of Piero della Francesca.

Gondolas

The gondola can be traced back to the mid-fifth century and is to Venice what the horse and cart are to Sicily, a signifier of local tradition. Gondolas are also associated with romantic love. The gondolier in his red-and-white striped jersey and straw hat serenades the lovers who have hired him while poling his boat through Venice's canals.

Middle Eastern Souvenirs

As in other regions of the world, small figures in national costume have become souvenir items in the Middle East. Distinct in the region are camels, whose images are sold as carved wooden forms with salt-and-pepper shakers on their backs. The coffee pot, a sign of hospitality, is an important icon of Middle Eastern identity. It can be seen in downtown Amman as a large sculpture-like monument in a public park, and it is sold in a small brass version as a souvenir.

Australian Souvenirs

Australians have had several sources of identity to draw on in creating souvenirs: their landscape, their fauna, and the culture of the Aborigines. The boomerang, an object that originated in Aboriginal culture, has been appropriated as a national Australian symbol. It has become the source of many souvenirs from ashtrays to ball point pens, while the koala bear and the kangaroo, in the forms of stuffed animals or salt and pepper shakers, function within Australian tourist iconography as alligators and flamingos do in Florida or the camel does in the Middle East.

Department
of Decorative Art

Many mass-produced objects are intended for home display and fulfill a similar function for the general public that expensive paintings and sculptures do for the wealthy. Almost everyone collects something and frequently the objects collected give an interior its character when they are displayed. In pejorative terms, this type of object has attracted such appellations as knickknack or tchotchke, which relegate it to minor status in the decorative arts hierarchy. But as corn-temporary art, these objects bear meanings for their owners who find in their iconography aspects of themselves. A pair of ceramic conga dancers, for example, might recall a sensuous moment in a couple's past. Such objects frequently take on distinctive identities within a home by the way they are displayed with other objects. In effect, one might be justified in calling such acts of display "vernacular exhibitions," a category that does not yet exist in the study of art.

Art Reproductions

Small statuettes of famous sculptures, such as Michelangelo's *David* or *Moses* or paintings like Boticelli's *Birth of Venus*, are like mass-produced print reproductions of art works except that the statuettes never preserve the proportions of the original figures because of the loss of scale. The Venus de Milo figures (lower right corner), as plastic salt-and-pepper shakers, take the appropriation of high art imagery one step further.

Mona Lisa Plate

Mona Lisa images are ubiquitous. They turn up endlessly in advertisements and appear regularly on mugs, key chains, tee-shirts, and dresses. Here, the Mona Lisa is applied to a small decorative plate in an attempt to give cultural credibility to an otherwise insignificant object.

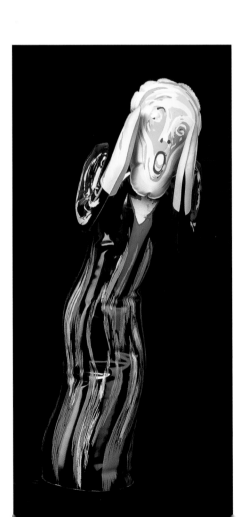

Munch's The Scream

The main figure from Edvard Munch's *The Scream* (1895) is here extracted from the original's frenetic background of swirling colors and transformed into an inflatable toy which undermines the figure's tragic import and makes it into a contemporary parody of the painting.

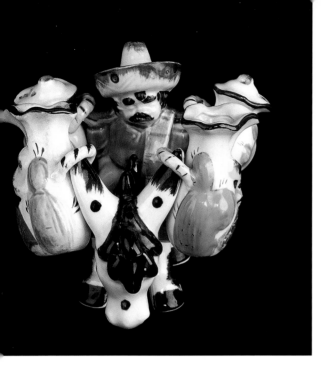

Mexican and Burro

Consumers in wealthy countries like the United States often pour their olive oil or salad dressing from jugs hanging from the back of a weighed down ceramic Mexican burro on their dinner table. If not in use, such objects may also grace living room shelves along with Chinese sages and Asian peasants astride teak water buffalos.

Red Bull

Following World War II, many American ceramic companies produced figures such as the red bull for home consumption. For a time these companies had the market to themselves but later they experienced stiff competition from foreign manufacturers, notably Japanese firms.

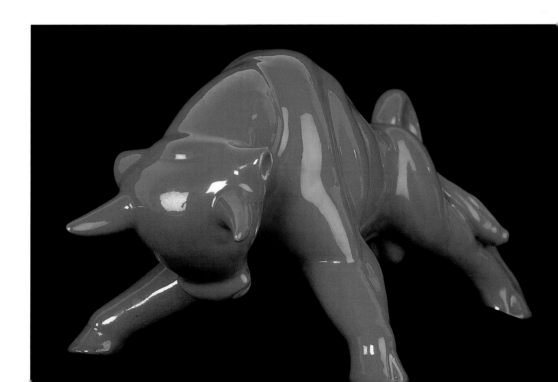

Outhouses

The outhouse is a classic icon of bathroom humor, which sometimes takes on the additional function of making fun of "Okies" or "hillbillies." Small texts on some salt and pepper shaker outhouses seek to provoke more mirth by punning on the comparable first letters of salt and pepper and pee and shit, as in "I'm full of P" or "I'm full of S."

Dogs and Fire Hydrants

One strain of American humor consists of jokes about the bodily functions of urinating and defecating. The dog peeing on a fire hydrant is a substitute for humans urinating in public and has historically been a source of humorous representations. An additional touch on some dogs is the fireman's hat, suggesting an analogy between the peeing animal and a fire hose.

Three Wise Monkeys, Sleeping Mexicans, and Monks

The origin of the Three Wise Monkeys ("see no evil," "hear no evil," "speak no evil") may well be traced to the seventeenth-century Toshogu Shrine, on which they appear, in Nikko, Japan, that serves as the mausoleum for the Tokugawa shogun, Ieyasu. Today the monkeys are sold more often as Chinese rather than Japanese popular culture. Frequently they are coupled with a fourth mischievous monkey and sometimes other figures are substituted for the monkeys such as monks or sleeping Mexicans, the latter figures having been produced in Occupied Japan.

Salt-and-Pepper Shakers

In 1540, Italian artist Benvenuto Cellini created an elaborate salt cellar for Francis I featuring the Roman mythological figures, Neptune and Earth. If we consider the salt cellar as a precursor of today's salt-and-pepper shakers, then it is not surprising that there is a continued taste for shakers that tell stories—as all of those depicted here do. Of course, the stories are not as lofty as tales of gods and mortals but this has not dampened the public's enthusiasm for pouring flavoring on their food from outhouses, caricatures of totem poles, and the heads of ethnic stereotypes.

Chinese Landscape in a Green Plastic Lozenge

A cultural disjuncture exists between the exotic Chinese landscape
inside this lozenge and the Day-Glo green plastic that encases it.

Asian Landscapes

Asian landscapes housed in small wooden or plastic frames are reminiscent of tranquil, classical Asian landscape paintings. They exist in great variety, with a vocabulary of objects—houses, trees, temples, birds—being used interchangeably to convey similar meanings.

Asian "Cute" Design

From the time the Japanese began manufacturing trinkets and souvenirs to revive their economy after World War II, diminutive child-like Asian couples such as those incorporated in these objects have been key icons. They represent an Asian aesthetic of "cute design" which can be seen today in artifacts from China, Japan, and Korea.

Japanese Geishas

The geisha is an icon of Japanese culture and her embodiment in small statuettes and figurines preserves her graceful gestures and elaborate hair style. In the three examples here, however, only one accentuates Japanese facial features while the others, most likely manufactured for export, depict the geisha with more Caucasian features.

Department of Folk Art

Folk art is a form of craft that suggests a lack of artistic training. What distinguishes it from the other objects in this collection is that it is not produced by machines. Each object is made by hand and various techniques are used—carving, carpentry, crocheting, knitting. Folk art is sometimes sold as tourist art, thus falling indirectly into the category of the souvenir, but it represents a different type of souvenir; not one that foregrounds a quintessential icon like the Statue of Liberty but one that functions as a trace of human creativity associated with a place. Folk artists manipulate materials according to their own inclinations and often idiosyncratic sensibilities. But folk art also falls into categories such as masks, quilts, soda can furniture, or crocheted shoes. Where such categories exist, one looks for the variation on the norm rather than the unique exemplar.

Shell Art

Shell art has become a genre in its own right and takes several forms. One technique is to make figures out of shells and another is to cover objects like salt-and-pepper shakers or plastic high heeled shoes with them. The latter results in new genres of folk objects such as shoes decorated with a great variety of shells and glitter or salt-and-pepper shakers covered with shells of different sizes and small or large colored rocks.

Gondola with Shells

The attention lavished on this decorative gondola suggests its importance in Venetian culture. The combination of colored crushed stone and shells gives its surfaces an ornate appearance, which differs from the sleek black paint on the originals. Though no lovers are shown, the folk gondola retains its association with "Italian" romance

Crocheted Shoes

The high heel, though worn less today, remains an icon of female sensuality. These high heel shoes, which are embroidered and then colored, represent an unusual striving for urban sophistication within a simple folk form.

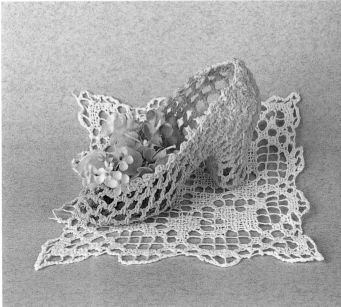

Mexican Wrestlers

Masked wrestlers are popular cultural icons in Mexico and are reproduced as plastic children's toys. Contemporary folk artists have painted these figures and installed them in homemade wrestling rings with the wrestlers' names painted on the sides.

Mexican Truck with Zapatistas

To raise money for their political struggle in Chiapas, Mexico, the Zapatistas have made wooden toy trucks with hooded figures in them holding guns. While not identified as such, one of the figures in this truck might well be the Zapatista leader, Sub Commander Marcos. The trucks have been sold in flea markets and related sites in Mexico. One even turned up as a background decorative object in the catalog of an American manufacturer of expensive brushed steel shelf brackets.

Cheka Figure

A curious subject for a hand-carved figure, this man is a member of the Cheka or Soviet secret police unit that was formed shortly after the Russian Revolution. The figure was acquired at the flea market in Ismailovo Park outside Moscow in the late 1980s and was more than likely carved around that time.

Soda Can Chairs

Cutting soda cans into strips and making small chairs and stools with them is a form of folk art with a long history. The rocking chair is a popular type as is the stool. Ornamental designs vary within a given style of curled strips, and frames are combined with small upholstered cushions. For art historical purposes, the style might be called Soda Can Baroque.

Chair and Stool

Miniature chairs are produced from other materials besides soda cans. This chair and stool were made with a material of a softer texture that invites curling and produces a less-disciplined aesthetic than those fashioned from aluminum.

Department of Commercial Art

Commercial art exists to promote specific businesses and products. It consists primarily of plastic or ceramic figures that are associated with merchandising displays, packaging, toys made by companies to remind customers of their products, and objects used in any other way to sell goods. Although these objects are produced for sales purposes, they have their own artistic qualities. Collectors have long been attracted to the small-scale statuettes that are used in store displays to promote specific products and these constitute a genre of their own. Packaging can also be artistic and anything from chocolates to scotch whiskey can be sold in a box or bottle that delights the eye and mind. Even the lowly swizzle stick invites aesthetic contemplation and can at times be the bearer of important cultural meaning.

Hot Dogs

The Oscar Meyer Company's Wienermobile, a truck-sized vehicle in the shape of an Oscar Meyer wiener was built in the early 1950s to promote the company's hot dogs on tours through the United States. Besides the full-sized vehicle, the company produced a small plastic wienermobile toy and wienermobile whistles. The Wienermobile in its various forms is part of a huge production of hot dog memorabilia ranging from erasers and salt and pepper shakers to plastic earrings.

Swizzle Sticks

The swizzle stick is normally overlooked as a bearer of cultural meaning. Although many do no more than advertise a hotel or bar with a banal image, some have more significance. Years ago, TWA chose a group of icons from Asian countries it had added to its Pacific route and reproduced them on swizzle sticks. The most notable was the dancing image of Lord Shiva seen in this display.

Greek Ouzo Bottles

Greek distilleries frequently adapt icons from classical Greek culture
such as columns and amphoras as packaging for their products.
While copies of amphoras and vases have been made since the
eighteenth-century, only recently have they served as containers for
liquor samples.

Department of Design

The world of designed objects is vast. Thousands of things are designed but only a few are collected by great museums of art or design. These institutions tend to focus on the most upscale products—fine furniture, sleek appliances, and elegant ceramics—but they ignore most of what is produced and consumed. They also tend to collect within a very narrow aesthetic range, primarily minimal modernism but now also excessive post-modernism with its arty pastiches of popular culture. Conversely, the Museum of Corn-temporary Art's Department of Design attends to those objects that would otherwise be forgotten by the great museums—thimbles, dog toys, coasters, egg cups, thermometers, and even wedding cake figurines. Whereas modernists prefer simplicity and post-modernists favore decoration, the Museum of Corn-temporary Art appreciates the storytelling qualities of most objects that people use.
Objects as icons—thermometers as Tyrolean huts, egg cups as nude bodies—are the stuff of everyday life and are enjoyed by more people than seek out Bauhaus chairs or Michael Graves hair dryers from Target.

Pens and Pencils

Pens in the shape of cucumbers, fish, or the Corcovado Christ from Rio de Janeiro are typical souvenir items that are often used for promotional purposes. Pens with tiny nudes floating inside clear plastic shafts are also erotic gag gifts.

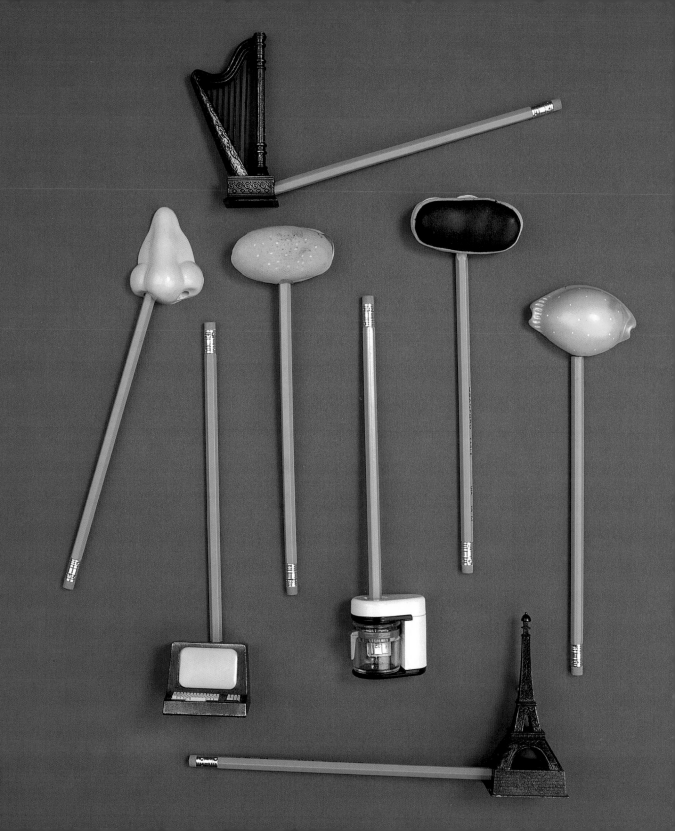

Pencil Sharpeners

Pencil sharpeners are functional objects that have yet to find their own contemporary form. As small metal buildings or monuments, they become another quiver in the souvenir seller's bow but many are produced as cheap throw-away products to fill the bins of Dollar Stores.

Thimbles

Images of Mammy and Uncle Mose have been widely used in decorative objects such as thimbles, salt-and-pepper shakers, and cookie jars since the 1920s. Surprisingly, they are highly priced objects in today's collectibles market and have provoked debate among scholars, both black and white, about their social meaning and value.

Tyrolean Thermometers

In Bavaria and the Austrian Tyrol, the thermometer attached to a chalet is frequently sold as a souvenir. Small plastic men and women in regional costume swing in and out of the chalet to indicate the weather.

Coasters

In the 1950s, women's breasts were displayed in popular objects such as coasters as an antidote to the conservative morals of that decade. These latex bosoms more efficiently grip the glasses than coasters or glass holders made of less flexible material.

Egg Cups

One imagines a couple in Birmingham or Leeds becoming aroused by these firm-bodied British egg cups from the '50s or '60s as they eat their boiled eggs. Perhaps the cups spice life up a bit when a woman eats her egg from the male one and vice versa.

Toledo Bull

The small lead bull, a souvenir of Toledo, Spain, contains metal swords that are used at cocktail parties to secure hors d'oeuvres, thus allowing party goers to imagine themselves as matadors while spearing an olive.

Dog Toy Hotdog

The rubber dog toy is yet to become the design icon of which it is capable. For the moment, many dog toys take forms such as fake human food like hot dogs and hamburgers.

Bush as Santa Claus

A manufacturer of rubber dog toys thought it would be amusing for his canine consumers to have a toy in the likeness of George Bush the Elder as Santa Claus.

White/Black Wedding Cake Figures

For years, wedding cake figures represented white brides and grooms but recently black figures have been put on the market. However, they are actually the same white figures whose skin is painted a darker color, thus perpetuating the old tradition of minstrelsy.

Wedding Cake Figures

Miniature figures of brides and grooms crown wedding cakes to signify the newlyweds' future happiness. It is not clear where or when the custom of putting these figures on wedding cakes began, although they can be traced back to the 1930s if not earlier. At first they were made of plaster but now most are plastic. A cynic might interpret the cheaper material as a sign of the reduced likelihood that the couple will stay together.

Department of Icons

Icons have strong political, religious, or cultural value. They serve a social purpose rather than function as decorative objects. Icons of political figures such as Mao Zhedong, Vladimir Lenin, Fidel Castro, and George Washington were produced to inspire public allegiance and national pride. Under repressive governments, it has sometimes been mandatory to have one in the home. In recent years, such icons have begun to circulate as collectibles outside the countries where the leaders lived. They have become part of a general commodification of political imagery that neutralizes the icons politically while at the same time extending their presence. Icons depicting cultural figures like Elvis, Marilyn Monroe, or the Beatles can easily become fetishes and the subjects of secular shrines, while religious iconography embodied in small objects brings the aura of the church or temple to the home, automobile, or other private space.

The Beatles

Here The Beatles are shown with the tight suits and haircuts from the first phase of their career just as some of their less adventurous fans like to remember them. By mounting each member's head on a little spring, the manufacturer instilled the group with mechanical life.

U.S. Presidents

Presidential likenesses have always found a ready market in the United States. The bust of George Washington is actually a bottle of men's cologne, which is revealed when the plastic head is removed.

Mao and Cultural Revolution Figures

During the Cultural Revolution in China, cheap plaster Mao statuettes were as plentiful as copies of Mao's Little Red Book. After the Cultural Revolution, they were harder to find but a new industry has recently sprung up in southern China to produce fake Mao memorabilia for the Hong Kong and Western market. The standing Mao figure at back right was purchased in China but the two busts and the Red Guard figures, picked up on Cat Street in Hong Kong, are more than likely recent fakes.

Fidel Castro and Che Guevara

After the Russians halted their sugar subsidies to Cuba, the government began to develop tourism as another means to bring in foreign revenue. Though enterprises by individuals are strictly regulated, vendors along the Malecon and in Old Havana sell home-made souvenirs to tourists. Among these are painted clay figurines of Fidel Castro and Che Guevara.

Che Souvenirs

The head of Che Guevara, taken from an image by the Cuban photographer Korda, has become the new Cuban logo. It appears on tee-shirts, which are sold at the fancy hotels, and on the cheap souvenirs to be found in public markets around Havana.

Ho Chi Minh Shrine

Small plastic shrine-like frames in Viet Nam
with photographs of Ho Chi Minh are sold on
the street today and keep alive the image of
the late Vietnamese leader.

Lenin Bust and Pins

Lenin busts, made of inexpensive plaster have been sold
for years in left-wing shops such as Collett's bookstore on
Charring Cross Road in London. With the disintegration of
the Soviet Union, their political charge has been defused
but they remain as material traces of Communist ideology.
For many years, Lenin pins have been collectibles and are
bought and sold at flea markets around the world.

Elvis

Elvis Presley is one of America's most popular cultural icons. He spawned a vast souvenir industry that ranges from tee-shirts and wall hangings to lamps, figurines, and busts. The plastic Elvis figure in this image was photographed against a backdrop that duplicates one of Elvis's most memorable stage sets.

Marilyn Monroe

As a small plastic figurine, Marilyn Monroe, the "blond bombshell," still exhudes the sexual allure for which she was famous.

Buddhas

Small carved images of the Buddha are standard objects in many households. Using the Buddha's image on a pair of salt-and-pepper shakers exoticizes Buddhism for Western consumption and undermines the figure's religious aura.

Saints, Marys, and Jesuses

Plastic religious figures function as miniature icons in the home or on the automobile dashboard. They serve as stimuli to affirm faith and evoke prayer. Some figures, more explicitly functional, are receptacles for holy water from Lourdes and other spiritual sites.

Department of Fashion

Corn-temporary fashion is difficult to define and a hard area to collect in. Thus far, the museum has concentrated on conventional garments and jewelry—tee shirts, ties, socks, and pins. Tee-shirts with parodies of paintings on them and socks and ties with high art iconography are examples of cornographic costume. The museum has a modest collection of these with a small selection of pins and earrings. There are also other possibilities that need to be explored, notably the way high fashion designers make use of folk and peasant clothing and the way techniques of high fashion have been incorporated into urban and rural folk styles of dress.

Socks Art

Socks art, which appropriates canonical Western paintings such as Grant Wood's *American Gothic* (1930) and Leonardo da Vinci's *Mona Lisa* (c. 1503–05), both of which are seen here, has affinities with the 1960s Sots Art movement in the Soviet Union, which parodied Social Realist paintings. A principal difference is that Socks Art has been appropriated as fashion, making it possible for consumers to turn their ankles into bearers of cultural meaning.

Ties

Tie art comes in many forms. Here, artworks such as Georges Seurat's Grand Jatte (1884-86), Piet Mondrian's paintings, and Pablo Picasso's figures have been appropriated as fashion-worthy decorations or patterns. The tie may also serve as a gallery for the display of pins and jewelry, such as the one here which pairs Che Guevara, the Cuban revolutionary, and Frida Kahlo, the Mexican artist, as one of the couples who might have been.

God and Moses Sock

The elegant transposition of Michelangelo's *Creation of Adam* (1508–12) from the Sistine Chapel to a pair of socks raises the question of whether the Italian artist might have been a successful fashion designer for Armani or Versace, if either been making clothing when he was alive.

Like Blid T-Shirt

"Like Blid" in Norwegian means something similar to "Keep Smiling." It seems that Edvard Munch's painting *The Scream* was weighing Norwegians down with its dour mood. The popular response was a T-shirt, sold on the streets of Oslo in 1994 to lift the national spirit.

Exhibits

The exhibits in this section, drawn from all of the museum's departments, were curated by Victor Margolin and Patty Carroll especially for *Culture Is Everywhere*. Patty Carroll designed all the installations. In putting these exhibits together, we adopted two different strategies. The first was to accumulate a great number of objects that exemplify a theme. Hence, The Many Forms of Feminity centers on a transparent female figure that establishes the biology of the body as a unifying force among diverse representations of femininity that stem from different cultures and for different purposes: a black cigar-smoking Cuban, a white Girl Scout, a kimono-clad Japanese, and even mythic figures such as Wonder Woman and Bat Girl. In this exhibit, realistic representations of women join with caricatures, mythic figures, and other forms to explore the many ways that femininity can be represented. Curating according to the accumulation strategy is expansive and does not limit the number or range of objects that can be included in a particular exhibit.

The second strategy we have followed is to place objects in settings or tableaux to tell a particular story. In the exhibit entitled Domesticity, for example, newlyweds come home to a domestic scene that is filled with incongruities. Framed by the scale of the doll house, small objects become large pieces of furniture, thus creating a curious domestic interior. Ceramic dogs loll about the house and shoes are dropped everywhere. Using the situation strategy, objects can assume narrative meanings that arise from the situations in which curators put them. Similarly, *Beach Scene* is a gathering of objects from different cultures that expose the realities of tropical vacations where visitors from well-off countries enjoy themselves in special tourist enclaves served by the locals who play the roles of happy natives to maintain the guests' fantasies of paradise. Such situations are highly charged with cultural meaning and suggest the possibility of many others that could be explored within the museum's collection. In fact, the exhibits presented here only begin to suggest how the museum's rich holdings can be used to investigate themes and issues of contemporary culture and life.

Shoe Tree

Miniature shoes have been manufactured for about 3,500 years and have taken on different meanings over time. Just as tiny Bibles were indicative of the printer's art, so did small shoes become signs of a shoemaker's skill. Miniature shoes have also symbolized, at various times, love, fertility, and prosperity. Besides their role as souvenirs, small porcelain women's shoes are among the most sought after contemporary collectibles.

Busts

The bust is an imposing form that suggests importance no matter who is being portrayed. Those included here, beginning in the back row, include Ludwig von Beethoven; António de Oliveira Salazar, former dictator of Portugal; Mao Zhedong; (middle row) Raden Adjeng Kartini, author of *Letters of a Javanese Princess* and a role model for Indonesian feminists; George Washington, William Shakespeare, Frederic Chopin, and Elvis Presley.

The Body

Collecting miniature body parts provides a safe release for unful-filled libidos. With regards to women, these parts take the form of big breasts—whether latex coasters which up the libidinal ante or ceramic salt and pepper shakers—while men are represented by big buns, broad chests, or bulging genitalia. Both sexes are attracted to foot feetishes in the guise of ashtrays or salt and pepper shakers. Fears of actual transgression are allayed by small plastic praying hands, which sustain the moral order.

The Many Forms of Femininity

Since the beginnings of art, "woman" has been a favorite theme of artists, yet
rarely has her nature been as thoroughly explored as it is here, where her representation ranges from icon (Wonder Woman, Marilyn Monroe) to role model (Girl
Scout, Choir Girl, Homemaker) to femme fatale (Scorpion). Chinese and Japanese
women are often shown as examples of "cute" design, which is a way of neutraliz-
ing their strengths.

The Many Forms of Masculinity

The male can be virile or boyish. He is a politician, a sage, a warrior, a laborer, or an airline host. A favorite masculine emblem is the boy who pees when you pull his plastic pants down, an icon of regression for all men who had repressed childhoods.

Chineseness

Chineseness has historically been expressed through various stereotypes ranging from Chinamen with pigtails to deities and "cute" child-like figures. It is easy to mistake these figures for those of another nationality since they do not always have distinct national costumes or other identifiable characteristics.

Mexicanidad

"Mexicanidad" or Mexican identity takes many forms, from a lively mariachi strumming his guitar to a sleeping Mexican. Folk art depicts men and women in their routines of daily life while a small plastic figure in sombrero and serape is an image of Mexican pride and revolutionary spirit. A Cuban guajiro, or cane cutter, has even managed to sneak into the picture. The skeleton figures are associated with the annual Day of the Dead.

Cowboy Boot Hill

Like the ten-gallon hat, the traditional leather cowboy boot is a sign of maleness. Artisans specialize in tooling and coloring the leather in complicated patterns, though sometimes exotic animal skins such as lizard are used instead. Special boots are also designed for women, though they are more petit. Miniature boots take the form of planters, salt and pepper shakers, small brass souvenirs, and even promotional plastic savings banks.

Indians

Despite years of treaties and consciousness raising, the image of the Native American as a "redskin" dies hard. Although most of these salt and pepper shakers, planters, and plastic toys are probably from the 1940s and 1950s, the "redskin" image still circulates as if it had no connection to contemporary realities. On the right is a more idealistic portrayal of the Indian, a small bronze reproduction of Cyrus Dallin's sculpture *Appeal to the Great Spirit*.

Buildings and Monuments

The miniature building or monument is perhaps the most identifiable souvenir of a tourist destination. Those shown here include examples from the United States, Europe, the Middle East, South America, Asia, and Australia.

Hats

Hats in Mexican, Texan, and Tex-Mex culture are frequently associated with machismo or "manliness." In much of Mexico, the sombrero, today worn primarily by mariachi musicians, is a tourist symbol of nationhood while in the north, the norteños, or Northerners, prefer headware that is more similar to the Texan's ten-gallon hat. These hats are also a favorite form for ashtrays in Mexico and southwest America. Folk hats in other cultures such as the four-pointed blue hat of the Sami (front center) or the straw hat of the Slovenian peasant (right-hand corner) also function as souvenirs.

Chairs

Small-scale furniture goes back to ancient times when it was placed, along with other objects, in the tombs of kings as possessions to take to the next world. Today, there are hand-made folk forms as well as diminutive mass- produced copies of classic modern furniture and traditional styles. Of all the furniture typologies, the chair, rather than the table, bed, or dresser, is most frequently reproduced.

Domesticity

The dollhouse usually depicts an immaculately neat domestic space of bygone days. Yet the dollhouse, as shown here, can also mirror more contemporary fantasies and tastes. The home of these newlyweds is filled with gargantuan tchotchkes. The American obsession with bathrooms is exemplified by four toilets while the dogs make themselves at home where they please and shoes are scattered willy-nilly around the premises.

Transportation

Transport is essential to the conduct of human life, and its various representations in miniature form serve as toys, souvenirs, and folk art. Folk artists tend to model more traditional and picturesque forms of transport such as bicycles, rickshaws, Chinese junks, and rickety buses while toy manufacturers go for the most contemporary vehicles.

Beach Scene

The beach, particularly if located on a Caribbean island, is a place of release. The more daring types sun themselves in the nude while others dance, embrace, and enjoy water sports. Smiling natives in the hire of hotels and resorts provide background music and proffer drinks to keep the good feelings flowing.

Curiouser and Curiouser: Looking through The Museum of Corn-temporary Art

Hannah Higgins

Seven years ago, while interviewing for a job at the University of Illinois at Chicago, I met Victor Margolin. He was dressed for a lecture on the Russian Constructivist, Kasimir Malevich. His black, white and red outfit spoke of a somewhat ironic relationship to the artist's work. He was as pretty as a picture. At a break in the interview, I was introduced to Margolin's collection. I met the China girls and sleeping Mexicans, toured the Egyptian Pyramids and the Acropolis, all at once and in a fraction of the time a real tour would take. Later, I would become one of the many who include Margolin on our list of giftees when traveling, and always with the greatest pleasure in deciding what, exactly, he is looking for. What, exactly, is this corny museum, anyway?

The Museum of Corn-temporary Art plays with our collective expectations for museums. Typical of parody, it moves between the domains of playfulness and seriousness by adopting enough of what is standard in museums to be recognized as such, while also poking fun at those standards. That is why the "museum" is organized into departments: the Department of Commercial Art, the Department of Design, the Department of Icons, of Fashion, of Folk Art, Decorative Art and Souvenirs. These department names are playful and irreverent, as is the attitude of Victor Margolin, who has coopted the departmental structure of museums while role playing the function of director. In summary, the Museum of Corn-temporary Art is a museum *about* museums and addresses how museums contain objects collected by tourists and fetishists of many kinds.

There is a long and respectable tradition of artists parodying the museum format. The first recent example dates to 1965, when Pop Artist, Claes Oldenburg, started a collection of found and mass-produced objects and assemblages (groups of these objects), which he called the Mouse Museum. In 1972, at the German art fair, Documenta V, a temporary Mouse Museum was built in the shape of the silhouette of Walt Disney's Mickey Mouse. The collection was then displayed at New York's Whitney Museum of American Art in October and November of 1978. By that time the Ray Gun part of the collection—objects with gun-like forms—had superceded its space in the museum. The Ray Gun Wing, in the form of a gun silhouette, was then added to the Mouse Museum. Oldenburg's museum parody, in other words, was founded, built, and expanded just like a traditional museum.

Like Claes Oldenburg, Victor Margolin rescues objects and puts them in a museum with thematic departments and an organizational structure. Rescuing objects has been an important function for museums historically. In each of these projects, Oldenburg and Margolin function like their nineteenth century forebears, collectors Ferdinand Franz Wallraf and the Boiserée brothers, who snatched up the work of Old German Masters left in the gutter after Napoleon's top art collector, Vivant Denon, had selected Italian Renaissance images from the Princes' collections.

Of course, the Boiserée brothers rescued work previously considered art, whereas the collectibles in Margolin's and Oldenburg's museums weren't art until they were displayed as art collections. The difference is significant. While all of these collections were culled from the streets, so to speak, the contemporary examples do not belong to the fine art media of painting, printmaking, or sculpture. Put differently, Margolin and Oldenburg have turned trash into fine art whereas traditional museums have often rescued fine art from the trash.

In the case of the Mouse Museum, however, this distinction is merely superficial. Since Oldenburg was an established Pop artist, one can assume a relationship to the category of "fine" art. The location of the museum in an artist's atelier, an art fair, and a major art museum provides the fine art context for the objects. The objects in the Mouse Museum also conformed to the display format of tastefully organized vitrines associated with fine art museums: "Through their placement in an orderly arrangement and separate from one another, with a overlapping here and there, they are able to maintain their own identity…their well considered placement in relation to one another brings out *the formal qualities of otherwise insignificant objects.*"[1]

As Margolin's introduction makes abundantly clear, the fine art museum context is almost entirely missing from his purpose, which instead serves the corn-temporary. The point of Margolin's collection is not to attune the world to the formal qualities inherent in these throw-away items as fine art, rather, to demonstrate the corn-temporary aesthetics of transformed materials—from everything else into plastic for the most part. Instead of a fine art collection, then, Margolin's museum might be better described as a collector's museum, as they are popularly known. Such museums house what have been called the collections of "normal" collectors: T-shirts, vehicles, miniature buildings, shoes, boats, salt-and-pepper shakers, guns, Disney memorabilia, etc. [2]

As a normal collection, the Museum of Corn-temporary Art resists the conventional logic behind collecting things of established or projected value, such as stamps in pre-packaged books or art by masters past or future. In contrast, it exists for the pure joy it brings the collector. As the critic Walter Grasskamp puts it, "the normal collector really is not quite so normal after all. Collecting appears in cases like this as a widespread form of deviant behavior…all that comes out of it is a collection. That collection may, however, be more bizarre and more fascinating than the results of artistic collecting."[3]

As Grasskamp suggests, collectors acquire a uniquely subversive function in the current cultural climate and "are restoring a lack of order to this overorganized, overtidy terrain [of the museum]; they are not only criticizing the canon of these scientific collections but they are also opposing the excessive sobriety and pedantry of the scientific form."[4] In the case of Margolin's museum, the flexibility of the exhibit formats, like his own wry humor, reflects a fundamentally creative (as opposed to aesthetic, documentary, or scientific) relationship to the materials. Parody and reverence coexist in an easy mix that seems to belie and oppose the fine art museum's practices of aesthetic presentation, codification, and classification. Unlike the Mouse Museum, the Museum of Corn-temporary Art renders elastic the codification and classification functions of official museums.

For the moment, Margolin's museum inhabits several sets of bookshelves in a third floor office at the University of Illinois at Chicago. The building's architecture is homely: concrete slabs, industrial shelving, neon lights, blue industrial carpet. No mouse-shaped or gun-shaped buildings. No Documenta. No Whitney Museum. No vitrines. Rather, it is the lucky prospective student or colleague who gets called into the Museum for a few minutes of free play. Unlike the Mouse Museum, which sought aesthetic and institutional affirmation, this museum and its director seem to hanker for something else: the joyful, fantastical, unpredictable, and living world of play.

Given its distance from the fine arts context, it may make more sense to look at another type of museum to understand how Margolin's museum is a museum about museums. The everyday nature of Margolin's travel articles, toys, and miniatures belongs to the natural history museum tradition, where travel to distant lands has yielded collections of artifacts of exotic nature and culture. The photographic dioramas constructed by the photographer Patty Carroll for this book establish little stage sets for these figurines that are reminiscent of the natural history museum diorama. In both situations, the diorama makes the viewer comfortable with, or naturalizes, the presented materials. The implications for the collections of Margolin's museum are ambiguous at best. The sleeping Mexicans, the China girls, and the black Mammy, to name a few examples, seem self-composed, naturally at home in, and seamlessly contained by their dioramas.

Writer Ann Reynolds describes the problem of natural history dioramas in precisely these terms: "The museum's artists achieved a high degree of illusionism in the groups through the use of sophisticated techniques…Illusionism, though, could not call too much attention to the elements that manufactured its mystery because they then would be revealed and their seductive power would be defeated."[5] In other words, the illusionistic diorama seduces the viewer into a passive acceptance of the situational milieu that, at least potentially, lulls him or her into an uncritical acceptance of the terms established by the situated object. The problem is aggravated by the fact that Patty Carroll is a fabulous photographer. These images are exquisitely crafted, extremely clever, and visually engaging. As a result of her skill, in other words, these politically charged objects are reproduced as mere stereotypes.

On site, however, in the university office of Director Margolin, the little objects function rather differently; there are no dioramas, just an ever-changing assembly of playthings and souvenirs. As a place that holds interactive exhibits, the museum suggests an engaged relationship to its materials. What's more, the exhibits are constantly revised, exposing new relationships, patterns, and possible modes of interdepartmental organization. This practice of imagining varieties of organization hearkens back to the serious and playful assembly of cabinets of curiosity in the sixteenth and seventeenth centuries. At that time, materials that are today classified as heterogeneous—minerals, animal specimens, suits of armor, magician's tools, religious icons, or bizarre plant life—were held together under one roof in these so-called cabinets of marvels.

In these cabinets, objects were organized sensually (by shape or texture) or by use value, religious association, or size. In other words, the links between objects were made without scientific knowledge, a proper sense of moral gravity, or an overarching intellectual scheme. The cabinet inhabited a home or office, its exploration constituting a form of wonderment and diversion. Margolin's museum is just such a cabinet of marvels. Its unassuming scale, which is largely obscured by the photographs in this book, makes it a clear descendent of these cabinets, which were introduced to the United States in Philadelphia by Charles Wilson Peale in 1786.

Because it is persistently expanded and reorganized in a myriad of ways that keep the collection *alive*, the Museum of Corn-tempoary Art illustrates by example what has been lost in the arcane process of refined categorization necessary to the mission of modern museums of all kinds. In point of fact, both the art museum and the museum of natural history have a common lineage in these cabinets of curiosities. As such, both of these museum types, like the cabinet of curiosities and Margolin's museum, bare explicit witness to the close link between travel and collecting.

In the eighteenth century, when Peale's cabinet was made and when the art museum and natural history museum were invented, travel was by boat and by horse. Going places was therefore more difficult, more time consuming, and more expensive. Compounding the problem, photography was nonexistent. For those who did not undertake the journey themselves, exotic places were known only through prints, drawings, written accounts and collections like Peale's.

In contrast to travel in this since-past Age of Exploration, tourism today reflects a broad-based democratization of the travel experience and the production of photographic records and of mass-produced mementos. Given this access to tourism and its artifacts, the places one travels to today are, to varying degrees, already familiar. Postcards and souvenirs now serve as mere affirmations to tourists and their associates that they have "been

there, done that." What's more, the objects can be purchased at home, online, in theme parks, thematic hotels and restaurants, as well as in second-hand and curio shops, flea markets and junk stores. The latter is particularly relevant to Victor Margolin's museum.

At various places and times, Margolin has selected a major thoroughfare and walked its entire length—the length of a city in some cases—to document and experience the abrupt and subtle shifts of culture and mood that attend to these passageways. These walks are highly structured, predicated as they are on the intersection of city planning and spontaneous commercial and residential development. The fabric of urban order—the grid-plan of scheduled thoroughfares—exposes its confounded relationship to its urban other, the unpredictable totality of modern, urban street life. Some of Margolin's objects have been purchased on these walks but most come from the similar contexts of flea markets and junk shops, those notoriously disorganized venues for the distribution of used and useless materials.

In other words, the objects in the Museum of Corn-temporary Art originate in the dustbins of our modern life, selected by an avid walker and witness to its energy, unpredictable encounters, and anarchic or undisciplined qualities. Margolin's walks point out the failure of a normalized, regulated traffic pattern to regulate *human* interaction, and are of a piece with his objects, whose unruly subject matter is difficult to contain within the fixed field of museum practice but which belongs to the topic of tourism.

Tourism expert Eric Cohen has identified different types of tourist experiences that range from the merely escapist, recreational type to the life changing and more culturally authentic, existential type.[6] These types are hierarchical and span the spectrum from mere pleasure to "the modern pilgrim in quest of meaning at somebody else's center."[7] For its supporters, mass tourism expands the cultural scope of travelers in a valuable, multi-cultural way. For its critics, the mass tourist visits sights prepared for his/her arrival with homey features that conceal the host culture's strangeness and relative discomforts, offering instead a palatable, if moderate, experience of generic newness. Attitudes toward mass tourism, in other words, span two poles concerning "the awakening of interest in the culture, social life and natural environment of others [and] a *generalized* interest in or appreciation of that which is different, strange or novel in comparison with what the traveler is acquainted with in his cultural world."[8]

The term "generalized interest" has negative associations primarily deriving from the seemingly superficial nature of this cultural exposure. As Cohen characterizes the debate, the recreational type of tourism produces the objects collected by Margolin, since tourist destinations are "characterized by mass trinketization, debased materials of local culture and cheap commercialization for tourist consumption."[9] For the proponent of tourism, however, these trinkets are produced cheaply and therefore constitute a kind of democratized curiosity cabinet, whose expensive and rare articles testify simultaneously to the adventurous spirit and class affiliation of their owner.

The subject matter selected for the tourist memento often reflects the perspective of the tourist vis-a-vis the tourist site. It is striking that the souvenirs of Western Europe tend to emphasize monuments of Western Civilization (the Pyramids, the Acropolis, the Eiffel Tower, the Statue of Liberty), all of which testify to the enshrined power of key sites in European history. Similarly represented are the shrines of civic religion (the Capitol, the Lincoln Monument in Washington D.C., or Lenin's Tomb), which signify stops on a political pilgrimage. In stark contrast, third world souvenirs distance the visitor from the everyday life and values of the first world. These collectibles tend toward quaint folk costume or representations of undisturbed nature. In every case, the chosen image is not monumental in character because the destination is not considered to have historic relevance.

Rather, third world and beach front mementos reflect the status of these destinations as appropriate to the recreational type of tourism. These places function as escapes from hectic everyday life for members of the first world urban elite. They are places without culture or, more precisely, without culture of significance for most tourists who visit them. Seemingly underdeveloped, these areas are fertile for the development of the tourist economy, an economy that no doubt contributes to the economic lives of these locations. As one critic notes, "It is important to investigate why it is that tourism, while bringing undoubted benefits to many poor countries, frequently also perpetuates already existing inequalities, economic problems and social tensions."[10] For the critic of tourism, the symbolic content of a collectible tourist artifact speaks volumes about the status of a particular locale's historic, civic, or recreational importance for the tourist.

The small, plastic curios, mass-produced crafts, and small-scale monuments in The Museum of Corn-temporary Art collection reflect this expansion of the tourist marketplace. Contrary to critics' claims, however, authenticity is not necessarily part of the experience of this collection, nor of tourism in general. The objective is free play, a good time, escape, and comfort. Large monuments can be reduced to pocket size and placed alongside other monuments on a shelf. Specific places may be exponentially expanded to include overlapping views of neighboring objects. In the Museum of Corn-temporary Art, the overlapping territory of tourist sites is virtually limitless, given the inclusive nature of the collection.

The objects in Margolin's museum and the dioramas that contain them are, in fact, miniature versions of the simulated cities at thematic hotels, such as Paris and Venice in Las Vegas. This occurs across the globe in the miniature Mexicos of Taco Bell, the wide ranging ethnicity of the Clud Med universe, and in Disney's Small World. What's more, because photographs frame objects, including some things and excluding others, our familiarity with tourist sites through photographic documentation means that we have a highly selective sense of what they are really like. As a result, the objects situated in the photographic dioramas in this book more closely resemble our expectations for the places they reference than the places themselves ever could, since the actual locations may be plagued by urban decay, poverty, and environmental damage.[11] The dioramas, in other words, represent an impossibly perfect world of fantasy.

Likewise—and far from limited to the means of representation—the photographs themselves, whose subject matter is politically incorrect, racial, and highly sexed, make associations with the world of fantasy unavoidable. The subject matter of the collection, as Margolin's introduction describes it, is forbidden, taboo, and largely impermissible in public discourse. The politically incorrect experience suggested by the objects demonstrates that by engaging with them, bizarre, fascinating, and productive encounters with situations and culture(s) are possible.

Volumes have been written about the fetishistic aspect of Western collecting habits in general, as well as collections of Asian erotica, academic and modern nudes, and sexually explicit nonwestern art. The rarified realm of the art museum largely obscures the seamy underside of the collector's practice. As a psychological necessity, the realm of fantasy is a necessary aspect of the adjustments routinely made by humans encountering their social system. To handle the breasts and body parts of the female fetishes, or even the shoe tree, in the Museum of Corn-temporary Art, in other words, is to give voice to the normal, even mundane, sexual functions of the socialized human animal. We repress them at our peril.

The fetish/fantasy playthings of The Museum of Corn-temporary Art—the shoes, the breasted salt shakers, and the Marilyns—belong to an imaginary framework that is no longer permissible in academic culture but which is routinely expressed in the popular culture which this museum collects. The diminutive sex objects shown in the Museum of Corn-temporary Art enable a kind of free play that potentially subverts this restrictive, politically correct, academic mechanism in a controlled and productive atmosphere. Professional museums systematically remove objects from interactive handling by visitors and fix exhibits in a manner that belies creative engagement with the objects. The Museum of Corn-temporary Art remarkably engenders both of these forms of interaction, traditionally omitted from the museum experience.

As it turns out, what has been driven out of the halls of the art museums and academic discourse has found a place in the exhibitionary order of everyday, commercial life. To ignore its appeal is to turn a blind eye to something that many people, privately or publicly, enjoy. The interactive Museum of Corn-temporary Art establishes a framework that invites users to simultaneously take pleasure in and critique its own collections as well as the various gender and racial presumptions that have produced these objects. And it does so in a manner which references the history of museums and how they collect: this is a museum about museums, and, even, about itself.

Hannah Higgins is Assistant Professor of Art History at the University of Illinois, Chicago and author of *Fluxus Experience*.

1   Claes Oldenburg, "Mouse Museum/Ray Gun Wing," in *Museums by Artists*, 266. Emphasis mine.
2   Removal from fine art is by degree only, as normal collections have also been included in several museum exhibitions including at the Musée des Arts Decoratifs in Paris and recent shows in New York of motorcycles in 2001 at the Guggenheim Museum and Jackie Onassus in 2002 at The Metropolitan Museum of Art. The French exhibitions are listed in Walter Grasskamp, "Artists and other Collectors," in *Museums by Artists*, 137.
3   Ibid., 138.
4   Grasskamp, 143.
5   Ann Reynolds, "Visual Stories," in *Visual Display*, Lynne Cooke and Peter Wollen, eds., (Seattle: Bay Press, 1995), 89-91.
6   Erik Cohen, "A Phenomenology of Touristic Experiences," in *The Sociology of Tourism* (London, Routledge), 94.
7   Ibid.
8   Ibid., 93.
9   Ibid.
10 Stephen Britton, "Tourism, Dependency and Development: A Mode of Analysis," 155.
11 This is precisely the form of experience recounted in Guy Debord's *Society of the Spectacle* and Umberto Eco's *Travels in Hyper-Reality*. See Guy Debord, *Society of the Spectacle* (Detroit: Black and Red, 1983) and Umberto Eco, *Travels in Hyper-Reality* (London: Picador, 1986).

The Museum as Corn-temporary Performance

Hermione Hartnagel

The motives and behavior of collectors have been extensively analyzed in the literature of psychology and psychoanalysis. Reasons for acquiring objects range from the child-like desire to incorporate the wonder of the world into one's own being to the more nefarious impulse of dominating through compulsive accumulation. Ernest Jones, Freud's biographer, asserted that

> All collectors are anal-erotics, and the objects collected are nearly always typical corpo-symbols: thus, money, coins (apart from current ones), stamps, eggs, butterflies…books, and even worthless things like pins, old newspapers, etc.[1]

Jones is equally suspicious of the feelings that collectors have for the objects they gather. "A more deifying manifestation of the same complex," he writes, "is the great affection that may be displayed for various symbolic objects. Not to speak of the fond care that may be lavished on a given collection."[2] Similarly, Otto Fenichel relates the collecting instinct to poor toilet training and suggests the possibility that what is collected may be a symbolic substitute for feces while the collecting instinct itself may be equated with the desire to hold back the elimination of bodily waste to allay fears of losing of control.[3]

Wilhelm Stekel, the Viennese psychotherapist, likens the collector to Don Juan who insatiably runs up an endless string of amorous conquests, although Stekel sees this acquisitive masculine impulse as a likely compensation for a man who in reality "may be an ascetic or the most faithful of husbands."[4] He also compares the way collectors choose their acquisitions to "the old struggle between polygamy and monogamy, between the idea of a harem and that of eternal fidelity."[5]

Psychoanalytic theory has become considerably liberalized since the days when all human acts were seen as either evidence of or compensation for unruly passions that moved deep within the self.[6] While it can still be helpful in exploring the collecting impulse, we can also see collecting, contrary to Jones and Fenichel, as more expressive than retentive. Stekel's equation of collecting with sexual conquest similarly focuses on the emotion behind obtaining the object rather than the intellectual pleasure of reflecting on it and displaying it. I am going to emphasis these latter functions in my discussion of Victor Margolin's Museum of Corn-temporary Art.

Margolin asserts in his introduction to this book that he has created a museum rather than a collection, a point which is essential to interpreting the array of objects he has amassed. He claims to be the director of the museum, as well as the curator of all the departments, and he additionally assumes the roles of education director, development officer, and head of public relations. The justification for his museum rests on his definition of corn-temporary art as a new object typology that has no place within existing museums. Margolin argues that corn-temporary art bears sufficient social meaning and aesthetic value to merit inclusion in a cultural institution. From his introduction, one concludes that his interest in corn-temporary art is both scholarly and connoisseurish. He provides no evidence of deeper drives that transcend the social and aesthetic, and his impetus to found a museum and direct its activities appears to be based soley on the desire to identify new categories of cultural artifacts and stimulate debate about their meaning.

In a recent interview, Margolin revealed that his collecting instinct first asserted itself when he was a child. He was an avid stamp collector and challenged himself by attempting to fill the largest stamp repository of his day, the Master Global Stamp Album, which purported to have a space for every stamp ever printed. Margolin states that he learned much of his geography and history as a stamp collector. He was fascinated by places with exotic names such as Azerbaijan, Guadeloupe, and Sierra Leone. At the time, he was completely unaware of geopolitics and appreciated the stamps for their iconography and formal attributes alone, although he did confess to a mild sexual arousal when acquiring a particular set of Austrian stamps with pictures of women in regional dress. Margolin also reported that he collected Lincoln pennies and combed eagerly through his change in search of rare items. At various times he also collected shells, and he had a collection of butterflies and beetles, which he mounted with pins in a cigar box. [7]

Despite his flirtations with nature, it was primarily cultural artifacts that fanned his collecting passions. The stamps received most of his attention, while he seems to have engaged in penny collecting in order to hone his collector's skills rather than attain psychic or intellectual satisfaction. What collecting pennies did show, however, was his inclination for serial collecting; that is, the amassing of all the exemplars in a given series or set of objects. This serial impulse is evident in his museum although it is only rarely associated with conventional typologies of collectibles and it is never taken to an extreme. More often it is a component of new collecting categories such as gondolas, Japanese women in bottles, or outhouses.

Before addressing the question of whether or not the Museum of Corn-temporary Art is actually a museum or simply a personal collection, I want to locate it within a tradition of museums created by artists. Perhaps the most closely related project to Margolin's is Pop artist Claes Oldenburg's Mouse Museum and Ray Gun Wing. Like Margolin, Oldenburg curated his own collection of small objects but he also designed buildings to house it. The plan of the Mouse Museum was based on the head of Mickey Mouse, while the Ray Gun Wing plan was shaped like a gun. The catalog of the Mouse Museum exhibition, held at Chicago's Museum of Contemporary Art in 1977, indicates that in 1965, when Oldenburg moved into a large loft at 14th St. and First Ave "[s]mall objects and fragments of man-made, artificial ("city") nature from different sources (found on the streets bought in stores, the residue of performances, souvenirs of travel, gifts, etc., etc.) which have accumulated and been carried along with works and furnishings from studio to studio are placed into a set of shelves found on the premises."[8] The objects in the Mouse Museum and Ray Gun Wing did not conform to any taxonomic standards of a museum. Oldenburg presented them as avatars of a new aesthetic of daily life, represented by cheap mass-produced products, found objects, both natural and mass produced, and small objects that he made himself.[9] Unlike the Museum of Contemporary Art, the principal aim of his collection was to challenge the museological conventions of high art rather than present a new typology of objects that carried a social meaning as well as an aesthetic one.[10] In his manifesto "I am for an art…," Oldenburg declared

> I am for an art that is put on and taken off like pants, which develops holes, like socks, which is eaten, like a piece of pie, or abandoned with great contempt, like a piece of shit.[11]

Another project that has affinities with Margolin's museum is Belgian artist Marcel Broodthaers's Musée d'Art Moderne: Département des Aigles (Museum of Modern Art: Department of Eagles). Where Oldenburg claimed to have converted his collection into a museum by designing buildings for it, Broodthaers made art about the administrative and curatorial practices of museums before he mounted an exhibition.[12] The opening of the Musée d'Art Moderne: Département des Aigles took place at Broodthaers's apartment in 1968 at a time when there was no collection. The inaugural address by Johannes Cladders, a German museum director, was followed by a discussion of art's relation to society. For a year, the apartment remained open as a museum, replete with numbered plaques and crates used for shipping artworks. Instead of real art being displayed, postcards with reproductions of paintings by nineteenth-century artists were taped to the wall. In 1972 Broodthaers mounted an actual exhibit at the Düsseldorf Kunsthalle entitled The Eagle from the Oligocene to the Present. It consisted of numerous representations of eagles, ranging from prints to sculptures, that were borrowed from forty-three international museums as well as from private collectors. The intent of the exhibit was to subvert conventional methods of classification by displaying the birds in a seemingly random manner. Broodthaers addressed the administrative and curatorial practices of museums rather than the content of their collections. The eagles he showed might well have been owls, frogs, or snakes. The point was to produce an event that brought into question the otherwise transparent institutional workings of museums.

The Mouse Museum/Ray Gun Wing and the Musée d'Art Moderne: Département des Aigles confront similar issues to those Margolin raises in his Museum of Corn-temporary Art. Other projects such as Herbert Distel's Museum of Drawers, a wooden box with drawers that contains five hundred miniature artworks by famous artists of the 1960s and 1970s, and Eduardo Paolozzi's *Kitsch Cabinet* of 1970, consisting of small mass-produced objects taken from his Krazy Kat Archives, fall short of the mark. Both maintain the high/low dichotomy that Margolin challenges with his concept of corn-temporary art.[13]

Whereas Oldenburg ironically housed his personal collection of objects in a mock museum and Broodthaers commented on museum practices by performing as a museum director and curator, Margolin purports to have founded an actual museum. He has a permanent collection, a system of classification, and a temporary home for the collection in his Chicago office. Is there any reason, then, not to treat this collection of corn-temporary art as a museum?

Let us first consider the ways in which the collection does not conform to the conventions of museum practice. First, almost all the objects are diminutive. This is not to say that other museums don't display small things. They do. For example, the new British Galleries at the Victoria and Albert Museum in London present objects in a range of scales from very small coins and seals to large period rooms. But the norm by which scale is measured is not the miniature. It is the traditional medium-sized decorative art object such as the silver bowl or Chippendale chair. In the Museum of Corn-temporary Art, almost everything is Lilliputian. This urges comparison with the world of the miniature and summons up images of dollhouses, electric trains, and toy cars. Critic and poet Susan Stewart views the miniature as a realm of escape from the harsh realities of life: "The miniature, linked to nostalgic versions of childhood and history, presents a diminutive and thereby manipulatable, version of experience, a version which is domesticated and protected from contamination."[14]

And yet the objects in Margolin's collection bear no relation to the nostalgic period furniture of the typical dollhouse, nor do they reference the small town architecture of an electric train set-up. His objects are confrontational. They are intended to challenge the viewer, to make her or him think about what they represent, whether sexual mores, racial attitudes, or political beliefs. In effect, the Museum of Corn-temporary Art presents big ideas in small forms. For that reason, it does not fit in the same category as the dollhouse. There is nothing nostalgic about the collection. It is polemical and very much about the present rather than the past.

The museum's objects just happen to be diminutive but they might have been much larger. Nonetheless, I still have difficulty calling the collection a museum, despite the fact that Margolin

has done his homework well. He knows the rhetoric of museums. He understands their systems of classification, and he is aware of the discourse on exhibition strategies. But the collection is just too physically inconsequential. And Margolin has not gone far enough as a museum director. He does not raise money. He has no board of directors and he holds no events. Nor does he have a fund for the new building he promises.

But, there *is* another way to think about the objects, particularly by bringing them back into relation with the projects of Oldenburg and Broodthaers. Oldenburg also deals in small things and only managed to achieve a larger sense of scale by designing buildings for them. But the Mouse Museum and Ray Gun Wing were housed inside Chicago's Museum of Contemporary Art and one could well argue that they functioned as props in a museological performance scripted by Oldenburg. By creating a museum inside a museum, he presented the Mouse Museum and Ray Gun Wing as if it were an actual institution, although the reduced scale of the objects and the buildings clearly contradicted this assertion.

Similarly, Broodthaers, without a building of his own, first housed his museum in his own apartment and meticulously acted out the role of director and curator to organize his initial opening. Whereas the objects in Oldenburg's collection were small in scale, those in Broodthaers' large exhibition, "The Eagle from the Oligocene to the Present," which was presented in the Düsseldorf Kunsthalle, were full-sized. The exhibit derived its museological reference from the fact that this curious collection of objects was presented with a rhetoric of display that belonged to a more conventional collection of paintings or sculpture. The disparity between the collection of eagles and the seriousness with which it was exhibited characterized Broodthaers' performance as its curator and promoter.

Both the Mouse Museum/Ray Gun Wing and the Musée d'Art Moderne: Département des Aigles provide the impetus to consider Margolin's Museum of Corn-temporary Art similarly as a performance. By performance, I don't mean the traditional definition of an artist, like the Futurist F. T. Marinetti using theatrical conventions such as histrionic gestures or provocative behavior to stimulate an audience, but rather a more contemporary notion, used by a number of artists like the German Joseph Beuys or the Fluxus artist Ben Vautier, of performing a role in everyday life that does not call attention to itself as theater. The contemporary approach to performance plays with a fluid boundary between actual behavior and acting.[15]

Margolin presents himself as the director and curator of the museum. He organizes the collection and manages the museum's public rhetoric but, as with Oldenburg and Broodthaers, the limitations of his project strongly suggest the performative. He is commenting on museum culture by playing the role of a museum director. Support for this reading also comes from what he has revealed about his childhood. As a boy, he was given a small theater with a velvet curtain and a stage with grooves in the floor along which he could move small lead figures. He has stated that he derived great pleasure from putting on plays with these figures.[16]

In what way, then, can we characterize the Museum of Corn-temporary Art as performance? First, there is the element of play. Margolin ironically exemplifies his objects as corn-temporary art. Although the reference is to objects that are "corny" or "trite," he presents them as serious representations of social values and mores. He also employs linguistic exaggeration by treating his objects as high art. Souvenirs, for example, are housed in a special Department of Souvenirs. Margolin organizes other parts of his collection according to the departmental nomenclature of established museums, thus he has a Department of Decorative Arts, a Department of Design, and a Department of Fashion. By creating a museological frame for objects that were never considered worthy of museum display, Margolin forces the viewer to challenge her or his prior responses to them. Unlike Oldenburg, Margolin asks that the objects in his collection be read as material evidence of social attitudes. He is not simply playing at being a museum director by grouping a collection of inconsequential objects into lofty-sounding departments whose semantic disjuncture with the objects they contain is apparent. He is serious about the objects' cultural import as well as the aesthetic strategies they embody.

At the same time, the Lilliputian scale of the objects is physically real and at first glance appears to undermine Margolin's assertion of their cultural value. But he may be compelling us to read the miniature in a new way. Polemics have always tended towards loud rhetoric and a large scale, whereas the idea of protest or argument at the scale of the miniature is a novel reversal of our expectations. If we are to accept this premise, then Margolin's performance is about much more than nostalgia or titillation. It becomes a drama tempered by irony and wit instead of a comedy weighed down by ponderous moralizing.

The dramatic aspect of the collection is enhanced by the geographic range of the objects, which contrasts sharply with the modest amount of physical space they occupy. They come from all parts of the world: North America and the Caribbean, Latin America, the Middle East, Asia, Eastern and Western Europe, and Australia. Many were obtained first-hand in those regions at flea markets, souvenir shops, and antique stalls from Cat Street in Hong Kong to Ismailovo Park in Moscow and the Lagunilla in Mexico City.[17] Margolin has already curated a few small shows with his collection beginning with one in 1991 that opposed the Gulf War. Using an old display case, he surrounded an anti-war pin with a ring of plastic soldiers whose rifles were directed at the pin. The title of the exhibit was *Defusing a Dangerous Idea*. He also lined up a fleet of McDonald's Happy Meal toys depicting smiling Muppets driving carrot-shaped cars and called it *Off to Fight the Gulf War*.[18]

Margolin has produced no manifesto as Oldenburg did nor has he manipulated the techniques of museum administration like Broodthaers. Besides the few modest exhibitions he has curated, his performance has been principally the rhetorical gesture of naming his collection a museum. With this act, he exaggerates the importance of his objects. But the paradox is that they really do carry social meanings, which, in fact, makes his gesture far more complex. Read simply as exaggeration, the gesture reduces the objects' significance. If we reject this reduction, we are faced with the conflict between his assertion of the objects' museum worthiness and the difficulty we have mapping our own museum experiences onto them. The objects thus appear as both meaningful and inconsequential. This is a clever feat on Margolin's part since the success of his performance as a museum director is predicated on the dissonance between what he claims and what we see. When that dissonance is challenged by our sense that the objects may actually be significant, we are thrown into a state of conflict, believing that we are having a museum experience when viewing the collection yet being unable to relate it to any museum experiences we have had before.

Because of this, Victor Margolin's collection of corn-temporary art packs a social punch. Margolin expands our received notions of where meaning can be found, locating it amidst the sprawling mass of the world's material culture, and he challenges the hierarchical aesthetics that prevail in the museum world. Though small, his objects loom large in our consciousness just as Margolin as a performing director and curator attracts our attention with a dramatic slight of hand in ways that few real museum directors and curators are able to do.

1   Ernest Jones, "Anal-Erotic Character Traits" in *Papers on Psycho-Analysis*, 5th ed. (London: Ballière, Tindall and Cox, 1950), 430. Cited in Susan M. Pearce, *Collecting in Contemporary Practice* (Walnut Creek, CA: Altamira Press, 1998), 127.

2   Ibid.

3   Otto Fenichel, *The Psychoanalytic Theory of Neurosis* (New York: Norton, 1945), 383. Cited in Pearce, *Collecting in Contemporary Practice,* 127.

4   Wilhelm Stekel, "The Collector" in Stekel, *Disguises of Love* (London: Kegan Paul, Trench, Trubner & Co., 1922), 56.

5   Ibid.

6   The negative view of collecting was not shared by Freud who amassed a sizeable collection of figurines and statuettes from ancient cultures. See John Forester, "'Mille e tre': Freud and Collecting," in *The Cultures of Collecting*, eds. John Elsner and Roger Cardinal (Cambridge: Harvard University Press, 1994), 224–251.

7   Interview with Victor Margolin, January 18, 2002.

8   Claes Oldenburg, *The Mouse Museum/The Ray Gun Wing: Two Collections/Two Buildings* (Chicago: Museum of Contemporary Art, 1978), 5.

9   When exhibited, the objects are grouped according to broad iconographic typologies—people, food, body parts, clothing, cigarettes, and cigars—as well as some formal typologies of Oldenburg's devising.

10 Curiously, some objects are duplicated in both the Mouse Museum and the Museum of Corn-temporary Art, although they are displayed with different intentions: a black plastic Venus de Milo pepper shaker, a plastic toilet, an outsized tooth brush, a fire hydrant pepper shaker, a ceramic hot dog salt shaker, a Washington Monument salt shaker, and a small replica of the Picasso sculpture in Chicago's Daley Plaza. The latter object reinforces the Chicago connection between the two collections.

11 Claes Oldenburg, "I am for an art…" in *Modern Dreams: The Rise and Fall and Rise of Pop* (Cambridge: MIT Press, 1988), 105.

12 The literature on Broodthaers is extensive. A brief account of his museum projects can be found in the exhibition catalog by Kynaston McShine, *The Museum as Muse: Artists Reflect* (New York: Museum of Modern Art, 1999), 62–69.

13 For a history of artists' collections and museums, see Walter Grasskamp, "Artists and Other Collectors" in *Museums by Artists,* ed. A. A. Bronson and Peggy Gale (Toronto: Art Metropole, c. 1983), 129–148. Sarat Maharaj discusses Paolozzi's *Kitsch Cabinet* in his article, "Pop Art's Pharmacies: Kitsch, Consumerist Objects and Signs, the 'Unmentionable'," *Art History* 15 no. 3 (September 1992): 334–350. See also *The Museum as Muse*, which documents a large number of museum projects by artists that were selected for a MoMA exhibition by that name.

14 Susan Stewart, *On Longing: Narratives of the Miniature, the Gigantic, the Souvenir, the Collection* (Durham and London: Duke University Press, 1993), 69.

15 See Rosa Lee Goldberg, *Performance Art: From Futurism to the Present,* revised and enlarged edition (New York: Harry N. Abrams, 1988, c. 1979).

16 Interview with Victor Margolin, January 18, 2002

17 Ibid.

18 Ibid.

Hermione Hartnagel is an independent critic and curator who has organized numerous exhibitions including *The Transgressive Tattoo* and *The Third World Bottle Cap*.

Suggestions for Further Reading

Collectibles

Larry Vincent Buster. *The Art and History of Black Memorabilia*. New York: Clarkson Potter, 2000.

Douglas Congdon-Martin. *Images in Black: 150 Years of Black Collectibles*. Westchester, PA.: Schiffer, 1990.

Thatcher Freund. *Objects of Desire: The Lives of Antiques and Those Who Pursue Them*. New York: Pantheon, 1993.

Kenneth W. Goings. *Mammy and Uncle Mose: Black Collectibles and American Stereotyping*. Bloomington: Indiana University Press, 1994.

Robert Heide and John Gilman. *Popular Art Deco: Depression Era Style and Design*. New York, London, and Paris: Abbeville Press, 1991.

Barbara Ifert. *Made in Japan Ceramic, 1921–1941*. Atglen, PA: Schiffer, 1994.

Sven A. Kirsten. *The Book of Tiki*. New York: Taschen Verlag, 2000.

Margaret Majua and David Weingarten. *Souvenir Buildings, Miniature Monuments: From the Collection of Ace Architects*. New York: Harry N. Abrams, 1996.

Leland and Crystal Payton. *Turned-On: Decorative Lamps of the 'Fifties*. New York: Abbeville Press, 1989.

Nancy N. Schiffer. *Imari, Satsuma and Other Japanese Export Ceramics*. Atglen, PA: Schiffer, 1997.

Milt Simpson. *Folk Erotica: Celebrating Centuries of Erotic Americana*. New York: Harper Collins, 1984.

Mary Rose Storey and David Bourdon, eds. *Mona Lisas*. New York: Abrams, 1980.

William Weaver. *America Eats: Forms of Edible Folk Art*. New York: Museum of American Folk Art, 1989.

Collecting

Russell Belk. *Collecting in a Consumerist Society*. London and New York: Routledge, 1995.

John Elsner and Roger Cardinal. *The Cultures of Collecting*. Cambridge: Harvard University Press, 1994.

John L. Marion. *The Best of Everything: The Insider's Guide to Collecting—For Every Taste and Every Budget*. New York: Simon and Schuster, 1989.

Susan M. Pearce. *Collecting in Contemporary Practice*. Walnut Creek, CA: Altamira Press, 1998.

Douglas and Elizabeth Rigby. *Lock, Stock and Barrel: The Story of Collecting*. Philadelphia, New York, London: J.B. Lippincott, 1944.

Kitsch and Camp

David Bergman, ed. *Camp Grounds: Style and Homosexuality*. Amherst: University of Massachusetts Press, 1993.

Matei Calinescu. »Kitsch« in *Five Faces of Modernity: Modernism, Avant-Garde, Decadence, Kitsch, Postmodernism*. Durham: Duke University Press, 1967.

Gillo Dorfles. *Kitsch: The World of Bad Taste*. New York: Universe Books, 1969.

Patrick Houlihan. *Indian Kitsch—The Use and Misuse of Indian Images*. Northland Press, 1979.

Jörg Huber, Martin Heller, Hans Ulrich Reck. *Imitationen: Nachahmung und Modell: Von der Lust am Falschen*. Basel: Stroemfeld/Roter Stern, 1989.

Barry Humphries. *Treasury of Australian Kitsch*. Melbourne: Macmillan, 1980.

Thomas Kulka. *Kitsch and Art*. University Park: Pennsylvania State University Press, 1996.

Liber Arce Matos and Fermin Galan Valdes. *Ole Kitsch*. Havana: Pinos Nuevos Ensayo, 1994.

Moles, Abraham A. *Le Kitsch: l'Art du Bonheur*. Paris: Mame, 1971.

Odd Nerdrum. *On Kitsch*. Oslo: Kagge Forlag, 2001.

Olalquiaga, Celeste. *The Artificial Kingdom: A Treasury of the Kitsch Experience*. London: Bloomsbury and New York: Pantheon, 1998.

Celeste Olaquiaga, *Megalopolis; Contemporary Cultural Sensibilities*. Minneapolis and Oxford, University of Minnesota Press, 1992.

Eva Pataki. *Haitian Painting: Art and Kitsch*. Jamaica Estates, N.Y.: E. Pataki, 1986.

Bernard Rosenberg and David Manning White. *Mass Culture*. Glencoe, IL: Free Press, 1957.

Susan Sontag. "On Camp" in *Against Interpretation and Other Essays*. New York: Farrar, Straus & Giroux ,1966.

Jacques Sternberg and Marina Henderson. *Kitsch*. London: Academy Editions and New York: St. Martin's Press, 1972.

Myra Yellin Outwater and Eric B. Outwater. *Florida Kitsch*. Atglen, PA: Schiffer, 1999.

Museums and Visual Display

Tony Bennett. *The Birth of the Museum: History, Theory, Politics*. London and New York: Routledge, 1995.

Lynne Cooke and Peter Wollen. *Visual Display: Culture Beyond Appearances*. New York: The New Press, 1995.

Kynastone McShine. *The Museum as Muse: Artists Reflect*. New York: Museum of Modern Art, 1999. (exhibition catalog)

Claes Oldenburg. *The Mouse Museum/The Ray Gun Wing: Two Collections/Two Buildings*. Chicago: Museum of Contemporary Art, 1978. (exhibition catalog)

Susan M. Pearce, ed. *Museum Studies in Material Culture*. London and New York: Routledge, 1995.

Kirk Varnedoe and Adam Gopnik. *High and Low: Modern Art, Popular Culture*. New York : Museum of Modern Art 1990. (exhibition catalog)

Peter Vergo, ed. *The New Museology*. London: Reaktion Books, 1989.

Museum Shops

Gottfried Fliedl, Ulrich Giersch, Martin Sturm, Rainer Zendron. *Wa(h)re Kunst: Der Museumshop als Wunderkammer: Theoretische Objekte, Fakes and Souvenirs*. Frankfurt: Anabas Verlag, 1996. (exhibition catalog)

Sam Weiner/Evangeline Tabasco. *Art Depot; An Exhibition Which Satirizes Museum Gift Shops and the Commodification of Art*. New York: Alternative Museum, 1994. (exhibition catalog)

Souvenirs

Nelson H. H. Graburn, ed. *Ethnic and Tourist Arts: Cultural Expressions from the Fourth World*. Berkeley, Los Angeles, and London: University of California Press, 1976.

Michael Hitchcock and Ken Teague, eds. *Souvenirs: The Material Culture of Tourism*. Aldershot: Ashgate, 2000.

Andreas Michaelis. *DDR Souvenirs*. Cologne: Taschen Verlag, 1994.

Ruth B. Phillips. *Trading Identities: The Souvenir in Native North American Art from the Northeast, 1700–1900*. Seattle: University of Washington Press, 1998.

Ruth B. Phillips and Christopher B. Steiner, *Unpacking Culture: Art and Commodity in Colonial and Postcolonial Worlds*. Berkeley, Los Angeles, and London: University of California Press, 1999.

Frank Stefano. *Pictorial Souvenirs & Commemoratives of North America*. New York: Dutton, 1976.